365

Most Prolific Motivating Quotes

From Today's and Yesterday's Leaders

Kevin H

Introduction

Life can be tough. We all go through our own challenges. Although we all want to be strong in the face of adversity, sometimes we just need a little bit of pick me up. The purpose of this book is to share with the world every tidbit of advice or motivation that has helped my friends and I through rough patches in life.

Every day for the past 10 years, I've kept a black notebook and jotted down anything anyone has ever said that has had an impact on my life. The quotes within this book have been gathered after sifting through thousands of books, video, and audio tapes. We have quoted famous authors, actors, artists, inventors, athletes, comedians, talk show hosts, Presidents, world leaders, celebrities, movie critics, and even billionaires. The common themes among all of the previous mentioned, is that each and every one of them have been successful in their own way. Each quote has its own interpretation.

How to Use this Book

Have you heard of the saying, "An apple a day keeps the doctor away."? What about, "A quote a day keeps you focused and ready."?

Read one quote a day. Take a couple minutes to digest the meaning of the quote. You may even write down a couple thoughts about it. Then write down the quote itself. Carry the quote with you for the remainder of the day. Your goal is to focus on that "lesson" for the day. For added bonus read the interpretation.

For example, day 9's quote is "Life only asks what you can handle." If suddenly you are burdened with a difficult or challenging situation, take out your sheet of paper and reread your quote. Remember that life wouldn't hand you a situation it didn't think you couldn't handle. Use this as motivation to help you get through your challenging situation.

Though this books is designed for you to read one quote a day. Alternatively you can haphazardly pick a quote based on the guidance you feel you need at any point in time.

365 Days of Prolific Motivating Quotes

Day 1

"People often say that motivation doesn't last. Well, neither does bathing. That's why we recommend it daily."

Zig Ziglar

Interpretation: Being motivated should not be a one-time thing. Daily repetition of good behaviors builds lasting habits. Motivate yourself daily.

Day 2

"To live is the rarest thing in the world. Most people exist, that is all."

Oscar Wilde

Interpretation: Just because you are here in the world, doesn't mean you are truly living life. Find what motivates, inspires, or moves you. If you are doing it right, you will feel alive.

Day 3

"Twenty years from now you will be more disappointed by the things that you didn't do than by the ones you did do, so throw off the bowlines, sail away from safe harbor, and catch the trade winds in your sails. Explore, Dream, Discover."

Mark Twain

Interpretation: Years from today, you will regret the chances you didn't take more than the chances you did take. Take a risk and follow your dreams. If it doesn't work out, chalk it up as experience.

Day 4

"Success consists of getting up just one more time than you fall."

Oliver Goldsmith

Interpretation: Persistence and patience will pay off in the long run. Keep your spirits up and keep at it.

Day 5

"Sometimes, things need to come undone for better things to come together."

Amy C.

Interpretation: Imagine you are in the middle of tying a tie. Halfway through you mess up; most people will just start from the beginning. Start from the beginning, you'll get it eventually.

Day 6

"What seems nasty, painful, evil can become a source of beauty, joy and strength, if faced with an open mind. Every moment is a golden one for him who has the vision to recognize it as such."

Henry Miller

Interpretation: Sometimes it's how you look at things. Keep an open mind and so will you let in the light on situations that may initially seem dark.

Day 7

"Get busy living or get busy dying."

Stephen King

Interpretation: If you aren't living then you are dying. Time is finite, if you aren't making the best of it then you are wasting it.

Day 8

"It isn't what you have, or who you are, or where you are, or what you are doing that makes you happy or unhappy. It is what you think about."

Dale Carnegie

Interpretation: How you perceive things is the difference between being happy or not. Federal min. wage in the U.S. is $7.5/hr, but in Botswana people would be thrilled as their wage is $0.58/hr.

Day 9

"Life only asks what you can handle."

Martha Kent

Interpretation: You'd be surprised what you can handle. Whenever you feel like life is overwhelming, just repeat the quote to yourself. Life presents you with challenges you can handle.

Day 10

"The only thing we have to fear is fear itself."

Franklin D. Roosevelt

Interpretation: You don't have to fear. For fear only exists in which you create or allow in your minds. In most cases, there is no point of being fearful.

Day 11

"Now what's it to be: The money...or your life?"

A Good Year

Interpretation: If you find yourself deciding whether or not to stay at work for an extra hour, ask yourself what you value. Yes, working harder may give you more money, but what about your life?

Day 12

"The grand essentials of happiness are: something to do, something to love, and something to hope for."

Allan K. Chalmers

Interpretation: Three keys of wisdom in life. Still I'd argue even if you don't have all three, you can still be happy with just one or two of the above mentioned.

Day 13

"The world bursts at the seams with people ready to tell you you're not good enough. On occasion, some may be correct. But do not do their work for them. Seek any job, ask anyone out; pursue any goal. Don't take it personally when they say "no" - they may not be smart enough to say "yes".

Keith Olbermann

Interpretation: There will always be people who tell you that you can't do something or that doing that something is not smart. Ignore the naysayers, do what is best for you and go after that goal you want.

Day 14

"Your life will become better by making others' lives better."

Will Smith

Interpretation: The secret in life is to make other people's life better. Only then will your life be better. Do something today to brighten someone's day. Give it a try.

Day 15

"Do not go where the path may lead, go instead where there is no path and leave a trail."

Ralph Waldo Emerson

Interpretation: Most of our early life is planned out for us. We go to elementary school, middle school, high school, and college. But, life is not supposed to be linear. Make your own path. It's your life.

Day 16

"Tough times never last, but tough people do."

Robert Schuller

Interpretation: You may feel like life is rough right now, but it will soon pass. You will come out of the situation stronger. Stay strong and you will get through it.

Day 17

"We must be the change we want to see."

Ghandi

Interpretation: You can't expect other people to change if you won't change yourself. Set an example for how you want the world to be.

Day 18

"Forget about correcting your past. You learn from your past as you go along. You can't say, If I had. . . . You say, OK, all right. That was a mistake. I won't do that again. That's how you learn."

Mel Brooks

Interpretation: Nobody can go back into the past and change what has already been done. All you can do is make the right choices today. Learn from your mistakes and move on.

Day 19

"As you breathe right now, another person takes his last. So stop complaining, and learn to live your life with what you got."

Anonymous

Interpretation: Remember that life is short. People leave all the time. Nobody knows when you will leave this Earth, so take advantage of your time here.

Day 20

"May you have the hindsight to know where you've been, the foresight to know where you're going, and the insight to know when you're going too far."

Irish Blessing

Interpretation: It's important to remember the past, but also to have goals for the future. But, don't lose sight of the important things in life by going overboard.

Day 21

"People do not decide to become extraordinary. They decide to accomplish extraordinary things."

Edmund Hillary

Interpretation: Focus on doing extraordinary things and you will be extraordinary. Focus on the journey and steps you need to take versus the end goal.

Day 22

"The amount of suffering in our lives reflects the gap between what we crave and what we have."

Roger Walsh

Interpretation: Temper your expectations. Be thankful for what you have and don't dwell on what you don't have. If you do this, you'll feel more at peace with yourself.

Day 23

Three Simple Rules:

1. If you don't go after what you want, you'll never have it.

2. If you don't ask, the answer will always be no.

3. If you don't step forward, you'll always be in the same spot.

Anonymous

Interpretation: If you want something in your life, you have to take a chance.

Day 24

"So go for what you want, ask questions, and take the one step forward because you never know where it might lead."

Anonymous

Interpretation: You won't know until you try. Take that first step and you won't regret it.

Day 25

"Socrates told us, the unexamined life is not worth living. I think he's calling for curiosity, more than knowledge. In every human society at all times and at all levels, the curious are at the leading edge."

Roger Ebert

Interpretation: Question life. Think outside of the box. Curiosity did not kill the cat. If we do not reexamine our lives, we will not have change from the status quo.

Day 26

"What is the difference between an obstacle and an opportunity? Our attitude toward it. Every opportunity has a difficulty and every difficulty has an opportunity."

J. Sidlow Baxter

Interpretation: Life is how you look at it. You decide whether or not you want to see something as an obstacle or an opportunity. Find the opportunity in the difficulty.

Day 27

"When you stop chasing the wrong things, you give the right things a chance to catch you."

Anonymous

Interpretation: The moment you figure out you are going after the wrong things, stop and pivot. You'll be surprised at the right things that start to catch up to you.

Day 28

"The present moment is the only time when real happiness can be experienced."

Brad Anastasia

Interpretation: Live in the moment. Learn from your past mistakes and move on. Focus on your actions today and it will take care of the future.

Day 29

"Try to stay flexible, open-minded, and skeptical."

John Templeton

Interpretation: Take life as it comes. There will be times when things go our way and other times things that don't. Go with the flow.

Day 30

"You aren't running away from who you are. You are running away from who you think you are becoming."

Clark Kent

Interpretation: Do you believe in destiny? Allow nothing to hold you back.

Day 31

"If you can find a path with no obstacles it probably doesn't lead anywhere."

Anonymous

Interpretation: Life is supposed to be difficult. You will encounter challenges and that's what makes life worth living. If it's easy you should be concerned.

Day 32

"Make mistakes of ambition and not mistakes of sloth. Develop the strength to do bold things, not to suffer."

Niccolo Machiavelli

Interpretation: It is better to be ambitious than to be lazy. If it isn't in your blood to be bold, develop it. You will be better off.

Day 33

"We were not put on this earth to work breathe and die. We are here to have fun."

Olivia Wilde

Interpretation: We work to live not live to work. Enjoy life because nobody on their death bed ever wished that they worked harder in life.

Day 34

"Holding on to anger is like grasping a hot coal with the intent of throwing it at someone else; you are the one who gets burned."

Anonymous

Interpretation: Learn to forgive. The more anger you bottle up, the angrier you will get. They can't feel that directly. In the end, you are doing yourself a disservice because you end up hurting yourself.

Day 35

"Amateurs sit and wait for inspiration while the rest of us just get up and go to work."

Stephen King

Interpretation: Become a professional. Find something you enjoy and can get up to work on without having to wait for inspiration.

Day 36

"Never burn bridges. Today's junior prick, tomorrow's senior partner!"

Katherine Parker (Sigourney Weaver), McGill's boss

Interpretation: You never know if your employee will be your boss one day. You may not think that it's possible now, but if it happens you'll be glad you didn't burn the bridge.

Day 37

"Learn from the mistakes of others. You can't live long enough to make them all yourself."

Eleanor Roosevelt

Interpretation: We can't make all the mistakes in the world. We don't have enough time to do that. Read and talk to others and learn from their mistakes.

Day 38

"You have to take the good with the bad, smile when you're sad, love what you've got and remember what you had. Always forgive but never forget, learn from your mistakes but never regret, people change, things go wrong, and just remember, life goes on."

Anonymous

Interpretation: Live life and go through life with your head held high. Be strong and humble. Learn from your mistakes and try not to have regrets. Things change and people move on, but so does life.

Day 39

"Develop into a lifelong self-learner through voracious reading cultivate curiosity and strive to become a little wiser every day."

Charlie Munger

Interpretation: Get better every day. If you are better today than you were yesterday, then you are on the right path.

Day 40

"I think that's the single best piece of advice: constantly think about how you could be doing things better and questioning yourself."

Elon Musk

Interpretation: There is always room for improvement. How you get ahead is to keep getting better whether it be professional, personally, or mentally.

Day 41

"The race is long, but in the end it's only with yourself."

Pick up dance

Interpretation: We compare and compete against other people in life, in the end you are only competing with yourself. People will come into your life, but also leave.

Day 42

"We are enriched not by what we possess, but by what we can do without."

Immanuel Kant

Interpretation: Less is more. The more material things you do without the more enriched you will feel. Cut away all your unnecessary distractions and focus on what is important.

Day 43

"Nothing can bring you peace but the triumph of principles."

Ralph Waldo Emerson

Interpretation: Do what is right. Only then will you be able to achieve peace.

Day 44

"Life does not come with a neatly designed manual. No one gives you a manual on trading when you start. You have to figure out things on your own."

Pradeep Bonde

Interpretation: There is no manual that tells you how to live life. For that fact, live life according to your own accord and not anyone else. Go through life and figure it out as you go.

Day 45

"Just remember, there's a right way and a wrong way to do everything and the wrong way is to keep trying to make everybody else do it the right way."

Colonel Potter

Interpretation: Few like to be told what to do. Avoid pointing the finger at others who need to change the way they are doing something. Allow them to come to their own realization of what works.

Day 46

"The size of your success is measured by the strength of your desire; the size of your dream; and how you handle disappointment along the way."

Robert Kiyosaki

Interpretation: If you want it bad enough, reach far enough, and dedicate yourself to that goal you will be successful.

Day 47

"If you don't do stupid things while you're young, you'll have nothing to smile about when you're old."

Anonymous

Interpretation: It is okay to make mistakes. It will give you something to laugh at when you are older.

Day 48

"Fear can hold you prisoner. Hope can set you free."

Stephen King

Interpretation: Fear can hold you back from what you want out of life. Think of the positive possibilities. Take that leap of faith and be hopeful.

Day 49

"To live an extraordinary life, you must resist an ordinary approach."

Frank McKinney

Interpretation: Take the path less traveled. That path will lead you on a journey that is out of the ordinary.

Day 50

"If you want your children to turn out well, spend twice as much time with them, and half as much money."

Abigail Van Buren

Interpretation: The biggest regret most parents have is missing their children's school activities. Kids don't care about how much money you have. They only care if you love them & spend time with them.

Day 51

"Never let the fear of striking out keep you from playing the game!"

Babe Ruth

Interpretation: Making mistakes and failing is part of the game. You can't win if you are afraid of failing. Don't let the fear of failing hold you back in life.

Day 52

"Success is really about being ready for the good opportunities that come before you. It is not to have a detailed plan about everything you're going to do, you can't plan innovation or inspiration, but you can be ready for it. And when you see it, you can jump on it and you can make a difference, as many of the people here have already done."

Eric Schmidt

Interpretation: Prepare yourself for when the opportunity arises you can take advantage of it. Take life in strides. Chances are you will be presented with different opportunities today vs. yesterday.

Day 53

"A wise man makes more opportunities than he finds."

Francis Bacon

Interpretation: Set yourself up for opportunities. Some opportunities will come to you, but if you are proactive you'll make even more opportunities.

Day 54

"Don't let regret take place of the dreams you have to chase."

Alan Jackson

Interpretation: Take action and go after what you want. One of the worst things that can happen is you look back and tell yourself that you wish you would've, could've, or should've. Do something now!

Day 55

"Life is a daring adventure or nothing at all."

Helen Keller

Interpretation: Life is about taking chances and riding the ups and downs. If you aren't taking chances then you aren't living. Just go for it.

Day 56

"There is little you can learn from doing nothing."

Zig Ziglar

Interpretation: You learn from your life's experiences. If you don't do anything, you will get nothing. Take action and deal with the consequences. It's part of life.

Day 57

"Even if you haven't encountered great success yet, there is no reason you can't bluff a little and act like you have. Confidence is a magnet in the best sense of the word."

Donald Trump

Interpretation: Fake it until you become it. One day you will make it, but until then do your best and your confidence will lead you to success.

Day 58

"Life isn't about finding yourself. It is about creating yourself."

George Shaw

Interpretation: You are not lost. You are right here reading this book. Make your own path in life, because that's what makes life worth living.

Day 59

"If you spend your whole life waiting for the storm, you'll never enjoy the sunshine."

Morris West

Interpretation: Worry less about what might happen and focus on the good and the positive or right now and right here. Most storms don't end up coming anyways.

Day 60

"How people treat you is their karma; how you react is yours."

Wayne Dyer

Interpretation: You can't control how other people behave or act towards you, but you can control your actions. Focus on your own reactions. Don't let their actions affect how you feel.

Day 61

"The friend in my adversity I shall cherish most. I can better trust those who helped to relieve the gloom of my dark hours than those who are so ready to enjoy with me the sunshine of my prosperity."

Ulyssess S. Grant

Interpretation: When it is going good, everyone wants to be your friend. But true friends are there when you deal with your deepest and darkest challenges/wounds.

Day 62

"Even on the road to hell, flowers can make you smile."

Deng Ming-Dao

Interpretation: Find the good and the positive in the dark storm. Stay positive because even in darkness there is light. You just need to see it.

Day 63

"In battle, discipline beats numbers 9 times out of 10."

Eddard Stark

Interpretation: When you are in a fight/battle, stay your course. Don't let emotions get the best of you. Don't get rattle. Just follow your plan and adjust as necessary, you will come out on top.

Day 64

"You will get all you want in life if you help enough other people get what they want."

Zig Ziglar

Interpretation: The secret to life is helping other get what they want. Only then will you get what you want. Sometimes the best route is the less intuitive one.

Day 65

"If we are facing in the right direction, all we have to do is keep on walking."

Buddhist Saying

Interpretation: Whenever you find yourself unsure of the path you are taking, think for a second and ask yourself are you going the right way. If you are then just keep going. Simple as that.

Day 66

"Go after your dreams no matter how unattainable others think it is."

Linda Mastandrea

Interpretation: There will always be people who don't think you can do it. But, forget about those people and go after what you want. It's your life. Don't let other people tell you what to do.

Day 67

"Success is not what you have, but who you are."

Bo Bennet

Interpretation: Material possessions never made a man or a woman. When all the glitz and glamour wears off, true character is revealed.

Day 68

"Keep your eyes on the stars and your feet on the ground."

Theodore Roosevelt

Interpretation: Shoot and reach for the stars, but stay grounded. Stay humble and don't let success get to your head. Be realistic, but aim high.

Day 69

"You may have occasion to possess or use material things, but the secret of life lies in never missing them."

Ghandi

Interpretation: Having less is more. Learn to live with less and you'll be happier and better off on the long run. That is the secret to life.

Day 70

"Smile. It enhances your face value."

Truvy Jones (Dolly Parton)

Interpretation: If this doesn't bring a smile to your face, then I don't know what will. Be positive and smile. You will feel better and be received better and everything else will follow.

Day 71

"The simple willingness to improvise is more vital, in the long run, than research."

Rolf Potts

Interpretation: Having the ability and willingness to pivot and go with the flow is important. Situations change and you'll need to adapt accordingly.

Day 72

"Work hard, be kind, and amazing things will happen."

Conan O'Brian

Interpretation: The keys to success is working hard and being kind. If you thank those who help you along the way and also put in the work, you'll be fine.

Day 73

"Everybody wants to be famous nobody wants to do the work."

Kevin Hart

Interpretation: If you don't do the work, you won't get what you want. You don't get to be successful by wanting something; you become successful by doing work.

Day 74

"Consider and reconsider the facts and your opinions. Stubbornness as to opinions must be entirely eliminated."

Bernard Baruch

Interpretation: Think critically and question the facts and your opinions. Our opinions can be wrong, it is important to pivot when you know your opinion is wrong.

Day 75

The adventure of life is to learn.

The purpose of life is to grow.

The nature of life is to change.

The challenge of life is to overcome.

The essence of life is to care.

The opportunity of life is to serve.

The secret of life is to dare.

The spice of life is to befriend.

The beauty of life is to give.

William Arthur Ward

Interpretation: Things will change in life and that is part of it. There will be ups and downs, but that is part of life. If you question what the purpose of life is, just read everything above.

Day 76

"I read it somewhere..how important it is in life no necessarily to be strong.. but to feel strong."

Christopher McCandless

Interpretation: If you think you are strong, you will feel strong. People can tell if you are confident or not. Remember it is just as much a mental thing as it is physical.

Day 77

"Don't think there are no beasts just because the forest is silent."

Paulo Coelho

Interpretation: Be cautious and prepared for the road ahead. Just because it looks like it will be clear sailing, doesn't mean you won't hit some bumps and get bruised along the way.

Day 78

"Many of my best growth experiences came about when I decided to connect with something that was important to me even when others disagreed with my choice."

Steve Pavlina

Interpretation: Do what you feel is important and not what others believe you should do. This is your life and you only live once. When you do what you feel is important, nothing else matters.

Day 79

"Where there is a will, there is a way."

Old English Proverb

Interpretation: In general, if you want it bad enough, you will do what you need to do to get it or get there. If you don't find a way then it means you don't want it bad enough.

Day 80

"When all the criteria are in balance, do the thing you least want to do. You have to decide early on whether you're playing for the fun or for the success. Whether you measure it in money or in some other way, to win at trading you have to be playing for the success."

William Eckhardt

Interpretation: It is better to make money than to be right. If your goal is to be successful, then your opinions shouldn't matter as much as doing what it takes to be successful.

Day 81

"Most spend too much time on what is urgent and not enough time on what is important."

Stephen Covey

Interpretation: Make a list and put your tasks and goals in two categories, label those categories 80%/20%. Put your "must do's" in the 80% category and the rest in 20%. Focus on the 80%.

Day 82

"Make it a great day or not, the choice is yours."

Anonymous

Interpretation: You decide whether or not you want to make it a great day or not. Your day will throw you curve balls, it depends how you handle them. Will you swing on a good pitch?

Day 83

"No intensity, no victory."

Christina Pagniacci (Cameron Diaz), owner of the Sharks, to D'Amato.

Interpretation: Put energy in tasks that you undertake. If you do that you will be setting yourself up for success and/or victory.

Day 84

"It is not the strongest of the species that survives, nor the most intelligent that survives. It is the one that is most adaptable to change."

Charles Darwin

Interpretation: Ten to fifteen years ago, if you knew how to use Microsoft Excel you were ahead of the game, now it is expected that you know how to use it. What's next? Learn programming.

Day 85

"Nothing will come of nothing. We must dare mighty things."

William Shakespeare

Interpretation: If you do nothing, you will get nothing and be nothing. Take action today and do what you normally wouldn't do. Take a chance and you might be pleasantly surprised.

Day 86

"The journey is what makes it so special and beautiful."

Pau Gasol on Lakers 2009 Championship

Interpretation: How you get somewhere is sometimes more important than your destination. Remember and appreciate the process as much as end results.

Day 87

"Don't go through life, grow through life."

Eric Butterworth

Interpretation: Strive to become better. Part of living through life is growing as a person. If you learn through your experiences, you'll be much better off.

Day 88

"Take life as it comes. Enjoy it and don't bother with regrets."

Anonymous

Interpretation: Take a moment to relax and go with the flow. Prepare for the future, but at the same time enjoy the present. My biggest regrets have always been having regrets. Avoid regrets at all costs.

Day 89

"Maybe you'll get everything you wished for. Maybe you'll get more than you ever could have imagined. Who knows where life will take you."

One Tree Hill

Interpretation: There's a possibility that you will get everything you wish for, but there's also a possibility that you won't. Not everyone gets what they wish for and that is okay. It's part of life.

Day 90

"You can't climb the ladder of success with your hands in your pocket."

Arnold Schwarzenegger

Interpretation: Nobody has gotten anywhere by doing nothing. Take action. Get off that couch and turn off that television, and go climb that ladder of success.

Day 91

"The best can't find you, until you put the worst behind you."

Anonymous

Interpretation: What is done is done. Learn from it and then put it behind you. You'll be much better off when you do and then you'll be ready for the best to come.

Day 92

"Our lives are defined by opportunities, even the ones we miss."

F. Scott Fitzgerald

Interpretation: There will be opportunities you take in life and opportunities you miss. Limit your losses and maximize the opportunities you do take. That's the way of life.

Day 93

"I never worry about the future, it comes soon enough."

Albert Einstein

Interpretation: Focus on the present. Soon days, weeks, and years will have gone by and you'll wonder where it all went. Work on the present and your future will take care of itself.

Day 94

"There are two kinds of people who lose money: those who know nothing and those who know everything."

Henry Kaufman

Interpretation: If you don't understand something, read, ask, learn about it. Educate yourself. Stay humble because you may think you know everything, but in actuality you do not.

Day 95

"If you want to be good at something, find someone that is good at what you want to do and do what they do."

Hank Haney

Interpretation: Learn from successful people. Successful people share similar habits, routines, characteristics, etc. Find what it is that made them successful, copy it, and then make it your own.

Day 96

"If you are afraid of failure you don't deserve to be successful!"

Charles Barkley

Interpretation: Don't be afraid to fail. We are all human and we all make mistakes. Many times failures come before successes. It's almost a precursor. Keep at it and you'll eventually be successful.

Day 97

"So when you're feeling kind of mixed up, just remember it's a mixed up world. And if you're feeling life is just too tough, just remember you're a really tough person."

Anonymous

Interpretation: Life is not supposed to be easy. It's not a fair world. There will be times when life is tough and you might feel down. But remember, to stay strong because you are a strong person.

Day 98

"Above all, try something."

Franklin Delano Roosevelt

Interpretation: Do something different. Just give it a shot. Who knows what will happen. You'll never know unless you try.

Day 99

"Next to knowing when to seize an opportunity, the most important thing in life is knowing when to forego an advantage."

Benjamin Disraeli

Interpretation: You can't have it all. It is knowing when and what to focus your energy on. Chase two rabbits catch none. Remember to not spread yourself too thin. Quality over quantity.

Day 100

"It's not about being the best. It's about being better than you were yesterday."

Anonymous

Interpretation: There can only be 1 person who can be truly the best. What are the odds that you are the next Tiger Woods or Michael Phelps? Play the odds and focus on being a better self.

Day 101

"Trust yourself no matter what anyone else thinks."

Arnold Schwarzenegger

Interpretation: Be confident in yourself. You know yourself the best and therefore you know what it is that you want out of life.

Day 102

"The price of anything is the amount of life you exchange for it."

Henry David Thoreau

Interpretation: How much life are you willing to trade for something? Think about that before you take that job where you will work yourself to death.

Day 103

"Do one thing that scares you every day"

Eleanor Roosevelt

Interpretation: The way to grow is to do new things and to face your fears. You'll get more out of life if you face your fears.

Day 104

"Marcus Aurelius hired a servant to walk behind him as he made his way through the Roman town square. And this servant's only job was to whisper in his ear when people praised him, You're only a man. You're only a man"

Jonas Cantrell in Law Abiding Citizen

Interpretation: When you do get that promotion, accolade, or praise, be humble because you are only a man or a woman. At the end of it all, we are all mortal and vulnerable at some point in our lives.

Day 105

"Either you run the day, or the day runs you."

Jim Rohn

Interpretation: Grab life by the horns. Take charge of your day or it will take charge of you. Be proactive today.

Day 106

"You can't cross the sea merely by standing and staring at the water."

Rabindranath Tagore

Interpretation: Take action now. You can't have what you want without doing what you need to do. An idea is just an idea until you act on it.

Day 107

"Every battle is won before it is ever fought!"

Sun Tzu

Interpretation: Prepare and visualize your plan before you take action. You'll have a better chance of winning than someone who hasn't prepared.

Day 108

"Education is a progressive discovery of our own ignorance"

Will Durant

Interpretation: The more you learn the more you find out you don't understand. Education never stops and it shouldn't. Keep learning and keep growing.

Day 109

"A goal is not always meant to be reached; it often serves simply as something to aim at."

Bruce Lee

Interpretation: Sometimes it's the journey that makes it all that special. It isn't always what you get at the end of it all. In fact, the path to your goal may prove to be more special than meeting your goal.

Day 110

"I think the people who succeed in life actually aren't necessary the best but are the ones who get up again and again."

Bear Grylls

Interpretation: The successful ones are those who keep trying even after failing over and over again. But they do it deliberately, by learning from their mistakes and avoiding the same mistakes.

Day 111

"Success is not counted by how high you have climbed but by how many people you brought with you."

Will Rose

Interpretation: It's not about you. It is about everyone else and what value you can bring to others and how you can help bring others with you on your path forward.

Day 112

"What's the worst that can happen?"

Tim Ferriss

Interpretation: The worst that can happen is you die. Luckily in most situations that isn't a possibility. What is it that you have to lose? You came into the world with nothing and you'll leave with nothing.

Day 113

"What you get by achieving your goals is not as important as what you become by achieving your goals."

Henry David Thoreau

Interpretation: Experience builds character. When employees hire you they look at experience. Why? Because they know you've gone through experiences that have made you who you are - valuable.

Day 114

"For after all, the best thing one can do when it is raining is let it rain."

Henry W. Longfellow

Interpretation: When you can't control something, the best thing to do is to let it be. There is no point in trying to control something that is out of your control. Worrying definitely won't change anything.

Day 115

"The secret of change is to focus all of your energy not on fighting the old, but on building the new."

Socrates

Interpretation: The past is in the past. Focus on the new and the future. We can talk about the past, but it's done and there is no going back.

Day 116

"If we fail to number our days, we risk waiting for things to happen instead of making them happen."

Karl Pillemer

Interpretation: When you're young, you think you have forever. When you become older you realize your time is limited. Then, it will be too late. All you are left with is a list of things you wanted to do.

Day 117

"One of the greatest weaknesses in most of us is our lack of faith in ourselves."

L. Tom Perry

Interpretation: You are more capable of doing great things than you initially are led to believe. You have the potential to go far; don't let anyone tell you otherwise.

Day 118

"The more you know who you are and what you want, the less you let things upset you"

Lost in Translation

Interpretation: Be certain of yourself and what you want out of life. You'll be able to focus on what is important and tune out all that noise. At the end of the day that's all that matters.

Day 119

"Nothing is permanent in this wicked world, not even our troubles"

Charles Chaplin

Interpretation: Having a bad week? It will pass and the weekend will be here. Before long you'll be back to normal. Come out alive and you'll be fine. Stay strong.

Day 120

"Check your ego at the door and check your gut."

Oprah Winfrey

Interpretation: Be humble and follow your gut. After all we are all only mortals. What does your gut tell you to do today? Quit your job? Live a fuller life? Change your habits?

Day 121

"The most beautiful people we have known are those who have known defeat, known suffering, known struggle, known loss, and have found their way out of those depths. These persons have an appreciation, sensitivity, and an understanding of life that fills them with compassion, gentleness, and a deep loving concern. Beautiful people do not just happen."

Elizabeth Kubler Ross

Interpretation: People who come out of tough situations are beautiful people. Just ask yourself why there is a rainbow after the rain stops and the sun shines. Tough experiences make stronger people.

Day 122

"You are too young to have any problems."

Edith Ross

Interpretation: When you look back to the problems you thought you had in high school, do you ever think of yourself "what was I thinking? That was nothing compared to the problems I face now."

Day 123

"Old patterns persist as long as they remain unchallenged."

Steve Pavlina

Interpretation: Habits are hard to change. Unless you make an effort to challenge them, your habits will continue to be. This also means it is less likely for your life to change. Good thing? You decide.

Day 124

"Remember that everyone you meet is afraid of something, loves something and has lost something."

H. Jackson Brown, Jr.

Interpretation: Everyone is mortal. No matter how high of a pedestal they seem to be on, just remember they too fear something and probably have been afraid of something at some point in time.

Day 125

"There is nothing amazing about being highly educated there is nothing amazing about being rich. Only when the individual has a warm heart do these attributes become worthwhile...When we reach beyond the confines of our narrow self-interest, our hearts become filled with strength."

Dalai Lama

Interpretation: Being rich or being highly educated is good, but it's not impressive. When you start thinking of others, caring about others, and putting others in front of yourself will you truly live life.

Day 126

"Hero is made in the moment not from questioning the past or fearing what is to come."

Brainiac

Interpretation: Live in the present. The past is done and the future is out of your control. Focus on the present and you'll be fine.

Day 127

"It's not about getting a chance, it's about taking a chance."

Anonymous

Interpretation: A chance is just a chance until you take it. Just like an opportunity is just an opportunity until you make something of it. Make your own opportunities.

Day 128

"I've learned that everyone wants to live on top of the mountain, but all the happiness and growth occurs while you're climbing it."

Anonymous

Interpretation: It is counterintuitive; you think you will be happy when you reach the top. But once you get there, you'll probably feel let down. When you do, just think about the journey you took.

Day 129

"If you want to be happy, be."

Leo Tolstoy

Interpretation: Simple as that. You chose to be happy or not. It's not what you have or what you don't have, but how you look at your life.

Day 130

"The stronger your belief in the uniqueness of each moment, the lower your potential to associate. The lower your potential to associate, the more open your mind will be to perceive what the market is offering you from its perspective."

Mark Douglas

Interpretation: Keep an open mind. Each moment is unique and offers different possibilities. Remember this and you'll be able to keep calm and reduce your stress.

Day 131

"But the least we can do - whatever activity we are involved in and whatever our circumstances may be- is to examine our motivation to be sure that our goal is not only of benefit to ourselves but also, and especially, of benefit to others."

Matthieu Ricard

Interpretation: The secret is to involve others in your successes. Ask yourself how what you are doing is benefiting others.

Day 132

"The only true failure is the failure of not trying."

Tony Clink

Interpretation: If you don't try then you will most certainly fail. It's a 100% fail rate right there. Think about it the next time you decide not to try something.

Day 133

"Leap and a net will appear."

Anonymous

Interpretation: Take a chance even when it looks like you have no fallback because when you do take that leap of faith, you'll find out that there was a safety net all along.

Day 134

"Stop regretting things and start accepting them. Our most significant opportunities will be found in times of greatest difficulty."

Anonymous

Interpretation: Regrets are things of the past. We can't change them, so the best thing to do is to accept them. Then look at the bright side, there will be other opportunities.

Day 135

"If you have something to say to someone, do it before it's too late."

Karl Pillemer

Interpretation: Life is short. If you've been meaning to tell someone something, do it today. Do it before it's too late.

Day 136

"Don't wait. The time will never be just right."

Napoleon Hill

Interpretation: If you keep waiting for the most optimal time to take that leap of faith and try something new or ask someone out, the best time may never come. Just do it.

Day 137

"The difference between a successful person and others is not lack of strength not a lack of knowledge but rather a lack of will."

Vince Lombardi

Interpretation: Where there is a will there is a way. Success is about how bad you want it and what you are willing to do to get there. Keep on truckin' along. You'll eventually get there.

Day 138

"Your time is limited, so don't waste it living someone else's life. Don't be trapped by dogma — which is living with the results of other people's thinking. Don't let the noise of others' opinions drown out your own inner voice. And most important, have the courage to follow your heart and intuition. They somehow already know what you truly want to become. Everything else is secondary."

Steve Jobs

Interpretation: Follow your heart and what your intuition tells you. There have been too many times when I've wanted to live up to other people's expectation, only to feel unfulfilled inside.

Day 139

"Named must you fear before banish it can"

Yoda

Interpretation: The first step of obliterating your fears is to identify it. Once you do that you'll be one step closer to getting over your fears. You can do it.

Day 140

"I'm not in this world to live up to your expectations and you're not in this world to live up to mine."

Bruce Lee

Interpretation: The purpose of life is not to fulfill other people's expectations. Live your own life by your own expectations.

Day 141

"Your present circumstances don't determine where you can go; they merely determine where you start."

Nido Qubein

Interpretation: The future is unknown and your current decisions can change it. Just because you may not be where you are, doesn't mean you won't get where you want to go.

Day 142

"Most of my major disappointments have turned out to be blessings in disguise. So whenever anything bad does happen to me, I kind of sit back and feel, well, if I give this enough time, it'll turn out that it was good, so I shant worry about it too much."

William Gaines

Interpretation: The next time you feel as if you've been disappointed, just remember that in a few days, weeks, or months you might be surprised to see that disappointment as a blessing.

Day 143

"There is no sunrise without sunset. There is no life without death. There is no success without failures."

T.T. Sidlow

Interpretation: You can't have the good without the bad. How else would you know something is good if you didn't have something to compare it to?

Day 144

"Fortune favors the brave."

Publius Terentius

Interpretation: Just based on sheer probability in itself, the more times you "play" the better chance you will win. The braver you are the more action you'll take. Eventually you'll hit.

Day 145

"Never let go of hope. One day you will see that it all has finally come together. What you have always wished for has finally come to be. You will look back and laugh at what has passed and you will ask yourself...How did I get through all of that? "

Anonymous

Interpretation: You can't connect the dots going forward only looking back. Trust in yourself and understand that as long as you keep making good decisions, eventually it will work out.

Day 146

"Too many of us are not living our dreams because we are living our fears."

Les Brown

Interpretation: Fear holds you back. While this might have been good when we were hunters and gatherers, in today's world this keeps us from experiencing new things that aren't life threatening.

Day 147

"Take things as they are. Punch when you have to punch. Kick when you have to kick."

Bruce Lee

Interpretation: As long as you do what you are supposed to do, you should be fine in the long run. When you feel stuck in your current job, do what you should do. Speak up or look for another job.

Day 148

"There is nothing more profitable for a [person than to take good counsel with [oneself] for even if the event turns out contrary to one's hope, still one's decision was right."

Herodotus

Interpretation: Follow your heart and gut. Do what you think is right. For if it doesn't go your way, at least you'll know that you did what you thought was right versus perhaps blaming others.

Day 149

"When you want something in life, you just gotta reach out and grab it."

Christopher McCandless

Interpretation: When you wanted that tablet and nobody gave it to you what did you do? You went out and bought one yourself. If you want something go and get it. This works with most things.

Day 150

"Not a single successful person ... has ever done great things because they played it safe."

Carson Kressley

Interpretation: To be successful means you have to be willing to take risks. While they need not be risk with unfavorable odds, you have to be able to take some kind of risk.

Day 151

"A journey of a thousand miles begins with a single step."

Lao Tzu

Interpretation: Rome wasn't built in a day. Google, Apple, Linkedin were all not built in a day. Take one step at a time and remember it's a long journey.

Day 152

"Everywhere I've been today there's always been something wrong--too young, too old, too short, too tall. Whatever the exception is, I can fix it. I can be older, I can be taller, I can be anything."

Foster, after being told he may not be right for the job.

Interpretation: Adaptability is the key to survival. Times are changing and so are skills needed to be successful. You need to find what you are good at or learn what skills are necessary in today's world.

Day 153

"The problem, simply put, is that we cannot choose everything simultaneously. So we live in danger of becoming paralyzed by indecision, terrified that every choice might be the wrong choice."

Elizabeth Gilbert

Interpretation: Face the music. You will make bad decisions once in a while. Make a decision, live with the consequences (good or bad), and move on. The future is always uncertain. No crystal ball here.

Day 154

"You think you can win on talent alone? Gentlemen, you don't have enough talent to win on talent alone."

Coach Herb Brooks (Kurt Russell) to team USA before their game against the Russians.

Interpretation: Talent alone is never enough. You will need to supplement it with effort. If you don't use what you have what good is having what you have? Nothing, it's unrealized potential.

Day 155

"There is no in-between. You are either a bystander or a difference maker in the face of changing trauma."

Devon Brooks

Interpretation: Which one do you want to be? Someone on the sidelines or a difference maker. If it were up to me, I'd be a difference maker. Be the change you want to see in the world.

Day 156

"At any given point you can release your greatest self. Don't let anyone hold you back. Don't let anyone dilute you. Don't be peer pressured into being less than you are. People willing to dilute themselves for the sake of others is one of the great tragedies of our time. Stop letting others define and set the pace for your life. Get out there and be your best. Do your best. Live your best. Make every day count and you'll see how exponentially more exciting, thrilling, successful, happy and full your life will be."

Steve Maraboli

Interpretation: Allow nothing to hold you back. Not your fears, your friends, your enemies, your family. Be the best you can be and make everything count. You'll be happier and so will those around you.

Day 157

"We can't predict the future, but we can certainly plan for it."

Michael Olguin

Interpretation: Knowing what to do or at the very least having an idea of what you should do should an opportunity arise will set you up better for success than if you didn't have a plan.

Day 158

"People rarely succeed unless they have fun in what they are doing."

Dale Carnegie

Interpretation: Most professional actors, actresses, athletes, and comedians enjoy what they do. So it is not a surprise that they are so successful.

Day 159

"Mistakes are always forgivable, if one has the courage to admit them."

Bruce Lee

Interpretation: If you own up to a mistake this means you acknowledge it. By acknowledging a mistake, this means you are more prepared to learn from it.

Day 160

"In three words I can sum up what I've learned about life: It goes on."

Robert Frost

Interpretation: You lost a PowerPoint presentation or a word document you worked on for two months. Now you have to start all over again. Oh well, life goes on.

Day 161

"You can play a much greater role than you thought in shaping your life and improving your lifestyle."

Herb Cohen

Interpretation: Don't underestimate what you can do with your life. You hold the cards and determine how you want to play them. Make it a great day or not, the choice is yours.

Day 162

"Good friends are like stars. You don't always see them, but you know they're always there!"

Old Saying

Interpretation: Be thankful for your friends. You'll know who they are when you need them the most. They will always be there even if they sometimes seem to disappear from time to time.

Day 163

"Nike is right: just do it. Learn what you can. Trust your instincts. Make your decision and go with it."

Harry Newton

Interpretation: Not sure if you should go for it or not? I have an answer for you. Just do it. Life is about experiences. If you don't have experiences then you can't say you are living.

Day 164

"Certain things catch your eye, but pursue only those that capture the heart."

Ancient Indian Proverb

Interpretation: Temptation is everywhere. There are things that catch your eye and peak your interest. How do you filter all of this information? Go after those things that move the heart.

Day 165

"Some of the best moments in life are the ones you can't tell anyone about."

Karl Pillemer

Interpretation: I'm thinking the moments you can't tell anyone about are moments that are illegal, intimate, or just too embarrassing. In any event, Karl says they are some of the best moments in life.

Day 166

"Strive to be authentic, not perfect."

Amy C.

Interpretation: Be true to yourself and genuine. Why try to be perfect when all it takes in life is to be authentic?

Day 167

"Learn every day, but especially from the experiences of others. It's cheaper!"

John Bogle

Interpretation: Looking for a new career? Ask someone in the field you are interested in. Looking to travel somewhere or try a new restaurant? Look up reviews or read about other's experiences.

Day 168

"Enjoy the little things, for one day you may look back and realize they were the big things."

Robert Brault

Interpretation: In life, every experience shapes you into the person you are today even the small things. Appreciate all things because you'll never know when the turning point was until you look back.

Day 169

"There is pleasure and there is bliss. Forgo the first to possess the second."

Buddha

Interpretation: Pleasure is temporary. Bliss is lasting. The first slice of chocolate cake will taste good, by the 3rd slice you start to not like it as much. On your 5th slice, you may be disgusted.

Day 170

"When you are content to be simply yourself and don't compare or compete everyone will respect you."

Lao Tzu

Interpretation: Be yourself and stop comparing yourself with others. Everyone is dealt a different hand in life. You can't expect to come out all the same.

Day 171

"We are in the business of making mistakes. The only difference between the winners and the losers is that the winners make small mistakes while the losers make big mistakes."

Ned Davis

Interpretation: Making mistakes is inevitable. The difference between those who succeed and those who don't is minimizing those mistakes. Learn from others to accelerate your learning curve.

Day 172

"Do not pray for easy lives. Pray to be stronger men."

John F. Kennedy

Interpretation: You can't control the hand you are dealt, but you can control how you play your hand. Work to be stronger every day and you'll be able to take on more than you ever imagined.

Day 173

"The best way to get started is to get started. Life rewards action - not reaction. Wait for nothing. Attack life."

Dave Kekich

Interpretation: Leave nothing for the swim back. The best thing you can do for your life is to do something. What are you waiting for?

Day 174

"A truly rich man is one whose children run into his arms when his hands are empty."

Anonymous

Interpretation: At the end of the day, your children won't care if you made $100k or $300k. They care whether or not you spent time with them, love them, and care for them. Be there for them.

Day 175

"Every single thing that has ever happened in your life is preparing you for the moment that is to come."

Oprah Winfrey

Interpretation: It's a given that we all learn from our experiences or ideally should. Just remember that each lesson is preparing you for the next exam.

Day 176

"Whether you fear it or not, disappointment will come. The beauty is that through disappointment you can gain clarity and with clarity comes conviction and true originality."

Conan O'Brian

Interpretation: Conan said it. It's inevitable. Disappointment will come, but the good thing is that as a result you may be able to gain invaluable insight, which will eventually lead to something new.

Day 177

"You can spend minutes, hours, days weeks, even months over analyzing a situation, trying to put the pieces together, justifying what could've, would've happened. Or you can just leave the pieces on the follow and move the f on."

Tupac

Interpretation: You may never get closure for the one that got away or fully understand why you failed. If you keep looking backwards, you'll end up living in the past. Or just move on.

Day 178

"If we relinquish our attachments by accepting what we have, the gap dissolves and so too does our unhappiness."

Roger Walsh

Interpretation: If everything we do is to become happier and you knew that accepting what you have will get you there, why would you want to do anything but relinquish your attachments?

Day 179

"If you can't find somethin' to live for, you best find somethin' to die for."

Tupac

Interpretation: What is your purpose in life? What do you want your life to mean? Will you just let it rot away or are you willing to do something about it?

Day 180

"Dreams don't work unless you do."

Anonymous

Interpretation: Everybody has dreams and not all of them come true. But the ones that do come true it's because they worked for it.

Day 181

"It wasn't raining when Noah built the ark."

Howard Ruff

Interpretation: Preparation. Preparation. Preparation. Anticipate what you'll need before you need it. Have an action plan. If you don't have a plan, then it doesn't matter where you go from here.

Day 182

"Minds are like parachutes, they only function when open."

Sir Thomas Dewar

Interpretation: Life is full of unexpected surprises. But if you aren't open to these surprises, you'll miss them. Keep an open mind and who knows what life's journey will send your way next!

Day 183

"If you want to test your memory, try to recall what you were worrying about one year ago today."

E. Joseph Cossman

Interpretation: The next time you worry about something, take a step back. Just remember that whatever it is that you are worrying about, it will soon pass.

Day 184

"If you risk something that is important to you for something that unimportant it just doesn't make sense."

Warren Buffet

Interpretation: While this may sound obvious, Buffet was referencing already successful individuals attempting to start a business hoping to make more money, while risking almost all their net worth.

Day 185

"No matter how good or bad you think life is, wake up each day and be thankful for life. Someone somewhere else is fighting to survive."

Interpretation: We often lose sight of how lucky we are. Take a step back today and count your blessings. Somewhere in the world someone is worse off than you are.

Day 186

"Why in the world would I be unhappy? People here complain all the time, but not me. It's my responsibility to be as happy as I can, right here, today."

Karl Pillemer

Interpretation: The responsibility to be happy lies solely on your shoulders. If you want to be happy, let yourself to be happy. Be as happy as you can right now.

Day 187

"If you want something said, ask a man if you want something done, ask a woman."

Margaret Thatcher

Interpretation: Most of the time we are all thunder and no rain. What does that mean? We talk, but we don't back it up with action. If you are a man, prove Margaret wrong. A woman? Prove her right.

Day 188

"Figure out what you want. Focus on it. Find people who have achieved what you want and find out how they think and act and then follow their lead."

Bill Harris

Interpretation: Go after what you want. Do everything possible to give yourself the best odds for success. This means spending time, talking to others, and learning from experts.

Day 189

"Pain is temporary; quitting is forever."

Lance Armstrong

Interpretation: Quitting is not in my dictionary. While you may feel terrible when you are in the heat of the battle, just know it will feel worse if you quit.

Day 190

"It is not the mountain we conquer, but ourselves."

Sir Edmund Hillary

Interpretation: Most things are fabricated in your head, so don't psyche yourself out. Keep it simple and stay focused.

Day 191

"The reason why worry kills more people than work is that more people worry than work."

Robert Frost

Interpretation: If you spend your time working, you won't have time worrying. Occupy your mind on what is important and it will not wander off to who knows where.

Day 192

"Don't be afraid to fail"

Arnold Schwarzenegger

Interpretation: If you are afraid to fail, you'll never take that leap of faith or that chance. That means your odds of success are 0%.

Day 193

"Confusion isn't a bad thing. It means you're growing and thinking."

Anonymous

Interpretation: Growth happens when you make a shift and enter uncharted territory. If you are unsure about where you are or where you are going, it's okay. You'll come out stronger.

Day 194

"If you love life, don't waste time, for time is what life is made up of."

Bruce Lee

Interpretation: We only have a limited time in this world. Our currency is not money, but time. We trade time for everything. Don't waste it today.

Day 195

"Stop yappin and start making it happen. All you gotta do is pick up the phone."

Terrell Owen

Interpretation: Isn't it ironic that Terrell Owen says that we should stop talking, but pick up the phone?

Day 196

"If you want something, go get it. Period"

Will Smith

Interpretation: Plain and simple. Go after what you want. There is nothing else to say; all that is left is to go after it.

Day 197

"Look. We both know life is short. Too short to waste a single second with anyone who doesn't appreciate and value you."

Sara Dessen

Interpretation: There are plenty of fish in the sea. Don't waste your time on those who don't care for you or don't appreciate you. You are worth more than that.

Day 198

"When you start off, you have to deal with the problems of failure. You need to be thick-skinned, to learn that not every project will survive. A freelance life, a life in the arts, is sometimes like putting messages in bottles, on a desert island, and hoping that someone will find one of your bottles and open it and read it, and put something in a bottle that will wash its way back to you: appreciation, or a commission, or money, or love. And you have to accept that you may put out a hundred things for every bottle that winds up coming back."

Neil Gaiman

Interpretation: The odds of success are almost always against you. If you know this you'll be better prepared mentally for future failures. But remember it only takes one bottle to wash your way.

Day 199

"Don't lose faith... You've got to find what you love. And that is as true for your work as it is for your lovers. Your work is going to fill a large part of your life, and the only way to be truly satisfied is to do what you believe is great work. And the only way to do great work is to love what you do."

Steve Jobs

Interpretation: At the end of the day, find what you love and you'll do great work. Don't get caught up on what others think and try not to worry about meeting other's expectations.

Day 200

"The man who can drive himself farther once the effort gets painful is the man who will win."

Roger Bannister

Interpretation: Most people drop off when the going gets tough, but if you are able to work through that you'll be that much closer to winning.

Day 201

"The secret of making dreams come true can be summarized in four C's. They are Curiosity, Confidence, Courage, and Constancy; and the greatest of these is Confidence."

Walt Disney

Interpretation: Be confident, courageous, consistent, and curious. Believe in what you are capable of doing and becoming. Work hard at it, don't be afraid to take risks and be curious.

Day 202

"Make it thy business to know thyself, which is the most difficult lesson in the world."

Miguel de Cervantes

Interpretation: You are positioned to learn more about yourself than anyone else can. The better you know yourself, the better you can identify your strengths and weakness and likes and dislikes.

Day 203

"In order to grow, you must repeatedly tackle fresh challenges and consider new ideas to give your mind fresh input."

Steve Pavlina

Interpretation: When you feel uncomfortable and out of your element. That is when you know that you are growing and learning. When you feel as if you are comfortable that's when you should worry.

Day 204

"No matter how hard the past, you can always begin again."

Buddha

Interpretation: There is always the next task, the next job, the next significant other or whatever. Know that you can always start over. It might not be easy, but know that you can always start again.

Day 205

"It does not matter how slowly you go as long as you do not stop."

Confucius

Interpretation: Slow and steady wins the race. Ride the trend and do what you need to do to get to where you need to get. As long as you keep moving you'll eventually get there. Don't give up.

Day 206

"Everything you want is on the other side of fear."

Jack Canfield

Interpretation: Whatever it is that you fear your reward is just behind it. Overcome your fears and you'll feel a great sense of satisfaction.

Day 207

"The pain of sacrifice is nothing compared to the pain of regret."

Anonymous

Interpretation: It may be difficult going through new experiences, but at least you can say you tried it or went through it. You don't have to wonder what if.

Day 208

"I can accept failure, everyone fails at something. But I can't accept not trying."

Michael Jordan

Interpretation: Words from the great Michael Jordan. Failure is part of growing and sometimes you can or can't control that. But what you can control is whether or not you try.

Day 209

"There's a moment where you're not a kid any more, when you realize time is finite."

Salman Rushdie

Interpretation: Time is limited. Think about how you want to spend it because it will be gone sooner than you think. Realize this sooner rather than later and you'll focus on what is more important to you.

Day 210

"My general attitude to life is to enjoy every minute of every day. I never do anything with a feeling of, 'Oh God, I've got to do this today'."

Richard Branson

Interpretation: You may say to yourself, well I'm not Richard Branson and I don't have the resources or financial means to do what I please. Think for a second. He was once financially like you and me.

Day 211

"There is no passion to be found playing small and settling for a life that is less than one you are capable of living."

Nelson Mandela

Interpretation: Realize your full potential. You are capable of so much more than that dead-end job or settling for that deadbeat significant other. Go big or go home. Only one life to live baby!

Day 212

"You may have to fight a battle more than once to win it."

Margaret Thatcher

Interpretation: You may not succeed your first go around, but that is normal. Keep on fighting and one day after you've learned from all your mistakes, you will come up on top.

Day 213

"There are times to stay put, and what you want will come to you, and there are times to go out into the world and find such a thing for yourself."

Lemony Snicket

Interpretation: When you find yourself staying put and things don't come to you, it is time to go out there and look for things. Know when you should be active or passive.

Day 214

"If you chase two rabbits, you catch none."

Confucius

Interpretation: Focus on more than one thing and you get distracted and lose focus. Despite what most people say, multitasking is counterproductive.

Day 215

"I make the most of all that comes and the least of all that goes."

Leo Sara Teasdale

Interpretation: Take advantage of opportunities that come by because they may not be here long. Leave the opportunities that have passed you by in the graveyard where they belong.

Day 216

"I don't know the key to success, but the key to failure is trying to please everybody."

Bill Cosby

Interpretation: It's impossible to try and please everyone. They all have their own ideals, fancies, and images of how things should be. You can't please them all, so just stop and listen to your heart.

Day 217

"He who says he can and he who says he can't are both usually right."

Confucius

Interpretation: Believe in yourself. If you don't think you can do something, then don't be surprised when you can't do it.

Day 218

"Flow with whatever is happening and let your mind be free. Stay centered by accepting whatever you are doing. This is the ultimate."

Chuang Tzu

Interpretation: Live in the moment and keep an open mind. Accept your current state of mind. Basically just start meditating, you'll feel better and live longer.

Day 219

"You don't get to choose how you're going to die. Or when. You can only decide how you're going to live. Now."

Joan Baez

Interpretation: There are a lot of things in life we can't control. What we can control is the decisions and actions we take now. Live life to the fullest and don't leave anything for the swim back.

Day 220

"Successful people are always looking for opportunities to help others. Unsuccessful people are always asking, 'What's in it for me?'"

Brian Tracy

Interpretation: Being successful is not about being self-centered. Help others and you'll end up helping yourself. You should be thinking, what is it in for them?

Day 221

"Work your butt off. Leave no stone unturned."

Arnold Schwarzenegger

Interpretation: Every opportunity that passes you by is a missed opportunity or an unturned stone. Don't be left wondering what was underneath that stone.

Day 222

"When I let go of what I am, I become what I might be."

Lao Tzu

Interpretation: Old habits don't change until you make a shift. They usually persist until they are challenged. Let go of your past and allow yourself to grow into the future.

Day 223

"The past is over - forget it. The future holds hope - reach for it."

Charles R. Swindoll

Interpretation: What is done is done. All you can do now is work on the present and plan for the future. Life moves on and so should you.

Day 224

"A smooth sea never made a skilled sailor."

Anonymous

Interpretation: Life is about going through challenges. There will be rocky roads and sometimes you might be pushed to your limit. But when you come out of it, you'll be that much more skilled.

Day 225

"The rain could turn to gold and still your thirst would not be quenched."

Buddha

Interpretation: Greed is a dangerous thing. The more things and money you have the more you want. It's human nature to want more resources, but less is more.

Day 226

"The true path to riches lies not with the wins, but managing the losses in a prudent, confrontational manner."

Mark Cook

Interpretation: Don't think for a second that successful people never lose. Their success lies in how they deal with those losses. Steve Jobs was once fired from his own company. Look at his legacy now.

Day 227

"Opportunities don't often come along. So, when they do, you have to grab them."

Audrey Hepburn

Interpretation: Some opportunities will work out and some of them won't. They don't come often and you won't know when the next one will come, so jump on opportunities.

Day 228

"You gain strength, courage, and confidence by every experience in which you stop to look fear in the face."

Eleanor Roosevelt

Interpretation: Have you ever played a game where all you do is level up your character? Think of life in that sense. Everything you go through makes you stronger. To get past certain levels you need exp.

Day 229

"My momma always said, "Life was like a box of chocolates. You never know what you're gonna get."

Forrest Gump

Interpretation: Expect the unexpected. You may think you know what life is going to be like, but things are constantly changing. There will be ups and downs, but weather the storm and you'll be fine.

Day 230

"For me, the most important thing in your life is to live your life with integrity and not to give in to peer pressure to try to be something that you're not. To live your life as an honest and compassionate person, to contribute in some way ... Follow your passion, stay true to yourself, never follow someone else's path, unless you're in the woods and you're lost, and you see a path. Then, by all means, you should follow that."

Ellen DeGeneres

Interpretation: Be you and do you. You may be swayed one way or another. At times it might be tempting to try and live up to other people's expectations, but it's better to be true to yourself.

Day 231

"However many holy words you read, however many you speak, what good will they do you if you don't act upon them?"

Buddha

Interpretation: These quotes are great for motivation and insight. But if you don't act on these lessons or insightful comments, what good is it all?

Day 232

"If you don't write your own rules someone else will and the results won't be pleasant."

James Altucher

Interpretation: You control how you want to live your life. If you don't put your foot down, then someone will walk all over you. They will then tell you how to feel, what to do, and how to live.

Day 233

"The purpose of life cannot possibly be waiting for Fridays."

Alan Jou

Interpretation: Some of us work and basically what we are saying is that we are willing to trade 4 ½ days for 2 ½ days of personal time. Find what you love and you won't feel like you ever worked.

Day 234

"There's no harm in hoping for the best as long as you're prepared for the worst."

Stephen King

Interpretation: Sometimes being too optimistic can set you up for disappointment. But if you know the worst case scenario and prepare for that, there's no reason for you not to be optimistic.

Day 235

"Every moment is a fresh beginning."

T.S. Eliot

Interpretation: At any moment in time, in theory, more than a billion scenarios can pan out. Keep your mind open and everything will look more uplifting.

Day 236

"Before you embark on a journey of revenge, dig two graves."

Confucius

Interpretation: There is no sense in seeking revenge. In this case, two negatives do not equal a positive. Give it time and think before you act. Otherwise you might end up hurting yourself.

Day 237

"It's only with the heart that one can see rightly; what is essentially is invisible to the eye."

The Little Prince

Interpretation: We often say things like "do what feels right in your heart" or "my brain says no, but my heart says yes". Do you ever wonder why? I think the heart has its own mind and it might be right.

Day 238

"Happiness is not something readymade. It comes from your own actions."

Dalai Lama

Interpretation: You aren't born with language skills; you had to practice to get better. Happiness is the same way. Meditate and cultivate happiness.

Day 239

"Pain is inevitable. Suffering is optional."

M. Kathleen Casey

Interpretation: Pain is merely an unpleasant feeling. Suffering is how you perceive a situation. You can be anywhere in the world, but if you have a negative outlook on life, you will be suffering inside.

Day 240

"Race your race and not the 'names' that may be next to you. They get dressed just like you do. They don't have 'super powers' and will be just as nervous and excited as you. Everyone is in the same boat at this meet. So just remember that, no matter what you see or hear, have a blast."

Amy Van Dyken

Interpretation: What do Elon Musk, Richard Branson, Warren Buffet, Larry Page, and yourself all have in common? All humans. You all don't have magic powers and aren't immune to fears and being hurt.

Day 241

"If you want to change somebody, don't preach to him. Set an example and shut up."

Jack LaLanne

Interpretation: Show not tell. Anyone can tell someone to do something, but it takes a certain person to walk the talk. You'll gain more respect that way.

Day 242

"I don't want to look back someday and regret that we wasted even one moment."

Corinne O'Kelly

Interpretation: Corinne was the wife of a Eugene O'Kelly a former KPMG CEO. He rarely took time off to spend with his family. While he had a great career, he almost lost sight of what was most important.

Day 243

"Discipline is choosing between what you want now and what you want most."

Anonymous

Interpretation: Would you rather have $100 now or $200 tomorrow? A study was done on children who had the discipline to wait for the $200. Years later those kids were more successful in life.

Day 244

"Peace comes from within. Do not seek it without."

Buddha

Interpretation: The truth of it all is that most things are how you look at it. If you view the situation as positive you will feel good. It's all mental and in your head.

Day 245

"There is only one question to ask yourself: "What would you do if you were not afraid?"

Anonymous

Interpretation: We know fear can hold you back. It's not enough to ask yourself the above question, but you need to act on it.

Day 246

"There's a redemptive power that making a choice has rather than feeling like you're an effect to all the things that are happening. Make a choice. Just decide what it's gonna be, who you're gonna be, how you are going to do it. Just decide. And from that point, the universe will get out of your way."

Will Smith

Interpretation: You have a choice in who you want to be and how you are going to do it. But, if you don't make that decision, the universe will make it for you. You might not like the decision it makes.

Day 247

"Set goals for yourself that are slightly out of reach, continually fail to achieve them, learn from your failures and never stop working your tail off to do better next time."

Cullen Roche

Interpretation: It's what you learn and what changes you for the better that ultimately will determine your success in life. Hard work and learning from mistakes = success.

Day 248

"If there's one thing I learned in prison it's that money is not the prime commodity in our lives..it's time."

Gordon Gekko

Interpretation: We all think money is the commodity we trade day in and day out, but it's really your time. How will you value your time?

Day 249

"Don't wait for the ship to come in - Swim out to it."

Anonymous

Interpretation: Unless there are sharks between the ship and yourself or don't know how to swim, you should swim out to it. Otherwise, I would just wait till the ship comes in.

Day 250

"No one is going to know or care about your failures. All you have to do is learn from them because all that matters is that you get it right once. Then everyone can tell you how lucky you were."

Mark Cuban

Interpretation: True story. If you don't believe me, do you remember any of Thomas Edison's failures to invent a light bulb? Enuff said. All we remember is that he invented the light bulb.

Day 251

"Your life changes the moment you make a new, congruent, and committed decision."

Anthony Robbins

Interpretation: Are you in a rut? Tired of the same ole same ole? Make a decision to quit your job, travel the world, or something. Your life will change when you make a committed decision.

Day 252

"Be decisive. A wrong decision is generally less disastrous than indecision."

Bernhard Langer

Interpretation: When you come to a fork in the road, make a decision, stick to it, and follow it through. This is much better than being wishy washy and not knowing flip flopping. Trust me.

Day 253

"If you look good, you'll feel good"

Kevin Hart

Interpretation: Dress up today. You know what happens when you dress up. You'll feel good. And if you feel good then it's all good.

Day 254

"A good life is when you assume nothing, do more, need less, smile often, dream big, laugh a lot, and realize how blessed you are."

Anonymous

Interpretation: Be thankful for what you have, give to others, be positive, and hope for the best. I could not have put it any better.

Day 255

"Once you replace negative thoughts with positive ones, you'll start having positive results."

Willie Nelson

Interpretation: Stay positive despite what negativity is out there. Personally, I would start by looking good. Then you'll feel good.

Day 256

"When you lose wealth, you lose nothing. When you lose health, you lose something. But when you lose you integrity, you lose everything."

J.W. McLean

Interpretation: I'd argue health is just as important as integrity if not more important. We are all humans in the world trying to live a good life. Look at it as if we are all in it together.

Day 257

"Whenever you find yourself on one side of the majority, it's time to pause and reflect."

Mark Twain

Interpretation: Be different. Think different. That's how the world evolves and grows. How do you think Steve Jobs changed the PC and computer industry? By doing what the majority did? Nope.

Day 258

"A failure is not always a mistake; it may simply be the best one can do under the circumstances. The real mistake is to stop trying."

B.F. Skinner

Interpretation: When if you first don't succeed, try and try again. Understand that your next attempt might be a successful attempt.

Day 259

"Try to leave life better than you found it."

Karl Malone

Interpretation: Perform a random act of kindness today. Say hello to a random stranger and try and brighten up their day. You'd be surprised by the after effects on how you feel.

Day 260

"If you do what you've always done, you'll get what you've always gotten."

Tony Robbins

Interpretation: This is basically saying that if you want something that you don't have you need to do something you've never done before.

Day 261

"A pessimist sees the difficulty in every opportunity; an optimist sees the opportunity in every difficulty."

Winston Churchill

Interpretation: How you view a situation will probably determine how you act on the situation. If you think something is impossible, then it will be impossible to you. But if you think otherwise…

Day 262

"Some men see things as they are and say why? I dream things that never were and say why not?"

George Bernard Shaw

Interpretation: A lot of people asked me what was my mind set for quitting my job. They thought it was ridiculous to leave a well-paid job. I told them straight in the face, why not?

Day 263

"Having a lot of money does not automatically make you a successful person. What you want is money and meaning. You want your work to be meaningful. Because meaning is what brings the real richness to your life. What you really want is to be surrounded by people you trust and treasure and by people who cherish you. That's when you're really rich."

Oprah Winfrey

Interpretation: There is a common misperception that money will bring happiness. That is of course the American dream, but I know people who don't have a lot of money and are truly rich.

Day 264

"Before you talk about what you want, really appreciate what you have before it's gone."

Ethan Daniel

Interpretation: We often don't appreciate what we have until it's gone. Don't make the same mistakes twice. Be grateful for what you have for it will not be there forever.

Day 265

"I'm a great believer in luck, and I find the harder I work, the more I have of it."

Thomas Jefferson

Interpretation: Life works in mysterious ways. Usually the harder the work, the more opportunities you set yourself up with. Isn't that funny?

Day 266

"The real opportunity for success lies within the person and not in the job."

Zig Ziglar

Interpretation: You can do anything in the world and be a success. The job doesn't necessarily determine whether or not you will be a success. There are successful artists just as there are doctors.

Day 267

"Every time we choose safety, we reinforce fear."

Cheri Huber

Interpretation: Stop being so safe. Take a risk and face your fears. Life is about living, not about trying to hide behind a shield.

Day 268

"If you hang around the barber shop long enough, eventually you'll get a haircut."

Denzel Washington

Interpretation: Work long enough in an industry and one day you'll get your big break. What Denzel doesn't say is that you have to improve. Otherwise your chances are the same as when you started.

Day 269

"Success is the sum of small efforts, repeated day in and day out."

Robert J. Collier

Interpretation: Contrary to popular belief, success doesn't happen overnight. It just so happens we find out about things overnight. But success comes from hard work day in and day out.

Day 270

"To get something you never had, you need to do something you never did."

Denzel Washington

Interpretation: Basically, this is saying if you keep doing the same things you'll keep getting the same results. Change it up and try something different.

Day 271

"The more I learn, the more I realize I don't know. The more I realize I don't know, the more I want to learn."

Albert Einstein

Interpretation: It's a never ending thirst for knowledge that led Einstein to be that successful in life. Never stop learning and growing. It's what makes us better people in general.

Day 272

"You can never cross the ocean until you lose sight of the shore."

Christopher Columbus

Interpretation: If you stick with what is safe, you'll never make it across to see what is on the other side. In Chris' case, he wouldn't have "discovered" the Americas.

Day 273

"I believe that one defines oneself by reinvention. To not be like your parents. To not be like your friends. To be yourself. To cut yourself out of stone."

Henry Rollins

Interpretation: Be unique. That's what makes each person so great. If everyone was the same then how boring would that be? Be true to yourself.

Day 274

"Remember that not getting what you want is sometimes a wonderful stroke of luck."

Dalai Lama

Interpretation: When one door closes another door opens. Sometimes that second door is actually a better door. It's okay if you don't get what you want, because it might be a blessing in disguise.

Day 275

"Perhaps we're too embarrassed to change or too frightened of the consequences of showing that we actually care. But why not risk it anyway? Begin today. Carry a random act of seemingly senseless kindness. Safe in the knowledge that one day, someone somewhere might do the same for you."

Princess Diana

Interpretation: Do unto others what you wish done to you or treat others how you would like to be treated. Be kind for one day someone might do the same to you.

Day 276

"It's not what you look at that matters, it's what you see."

Henry David Thoreau

Interpretation: A beautiful woman may be a mate to a man, but a meal to a lion. It's not what you look at, but what you see. Open your eyes.

Day 277

"If you're not making someone else's life better, you're wasting your time."

Will Smith

Interpretation: In all honestly, the times when I've felt the best was when I've helped others and made their life better. It always feels good when you feel like you had an impact on someone's life.

Day 278

"This above all: to your own self be true."

William Shakespeare

Interpretation: Be true to yourself is not a new concept. The problem is that some of us don't know ourselves well enough to be true to ourselves, so we end up living up to others' standards.

Day 279

"When the need to succeed is as bad as the need to breathe, then you'll be successful."

Eric Thomas

Interpretation: How bad do you want something? If you want it bad enough then you'll succeed. If you don't succeed then that means you didn't want it bad enough.

Day 280

"You know what money can't buy? What you have now. Life."

Kenshin

Interpretation: The next time you think about trying to be a millionaire or billionaire, think of what money can't buy. That is life, which you already have.

Day 281

"It matters how you are going to finish. Are you going to finish strong?"

Nick Vijicic

Interpretation: You are nearing the end of the race, don't give up. Finish strong you are tired now, but will thank me later.

Day 282

"In the end, we only regret the chances we didn't take, relationships we were afraid to have, and the decisions we waited too long to make."

Anonymous

Interpretation: Most of the time it is better to take the risk and deal with the consequences than be afraid and wish what could've, should've, would've happened. That's the worst feeling.

Day 283

"You can never be who you want to be if you are always looking over your shoulder at what could've been."

Chloe from Smallville

Interpretation: If you keep living in the past, then you'll never focus on the present and the future. Move on or life will move on without you.

Day 284

"About all you can do in life is be who you are. Some people will love you for you. Most will love you for what you can do for them, and some won't like you at all."

Rita Mae Brown

Interpretation: You can't be loved and adored by everyone. Be yourself. It's okay if people don't like you because there will also be people who do like you. That's life. Deal with it.

Day 285

"Your attitude, not your aptitude, will determine your altitude."

Zig Ziglar

Interpretation: How far you go in life is more about your attitude then it is about how smart you are. Would you rather be around someone who is constantly negative or someone who is positive?

Day 286

"Learn your lessons quickly and move on."

Eileen Caddy

Interpretation: The hardest thing in life is letting go of what could've been. But, you live and learn. The faster you are able to learn from it and move on the better off you'll be. We can't change the past.

Day 287

"Remember, YOU can only do YOUR best. If someone else can't appreciate that, it's THEIR problem, not yours."

Anonymous

Interpretation: If you do your best, then what else is there to ask of yourself? You can't do any better than your best. If it's not good enough for someone else then, there's nothing you can do anyways.

Day 288

"There will always be people in your life, who hold you back, who cost you too much, and who fail to see all you've done for them. But, of course they're just there to teach you that you do have time, that you'll always be rich, and that your own high standard are all that matter. Sounds like a good deal to me."

Anonymous

Interpretation: You won't always get back what you give. Of course there will always be people who try to bring you down and not appreciate you. Its okay, your own standards are all that matter.

Day 289

"If you're not swerving around and hitting the guard rails every now and then, you're not going fast enough. Your biggest risk isn't failing, it's being too comfortable."

Drew Houston

Interpretation: Be reckless. I'm just kidding. Life has enough challenges; we don't need to go around making waves, right? Well just make sure you have some waves, otherwise life isn't worth living.

Day 290

"Life is simple. You make choices and you don't look back."

Sung Kang

Interpretation: This is a great quote for whenever I have a hard time making a decision. Usually after reading this, I make a decision and move on.

Day 291

"If you've got a great idea, if you can improve people's lives, just go on and do it. I have a phrase -- 'Screw it. Just do it.'."

Richard Branson

Interpretation: Seems pretty straightforward to me. If it helps others then you should create and bring this product or service to life.

Day 292

"Let others lead small lives, but not you. Let others argue over small things, but not you. Let others cry over small hurts, but not you. Let others leave their future in someone else's hands, but not you."

Jim Rohn

Interpretation: Be the bigger man or woman. Be proactive over your life and don't sweat the small stuff. It's not worth it.

Day 293

"If opportunity doesn't knock, build a door."

Milton Berle

Interpretation: Make your own opportunities if they don't come to you. Where there is a will there is a way. You'll be surprised what you can do.

Day 294

"It is better to risk everything than to hold on to nothing."

Clark Kent

Interpretation: The difficulty lies in figuring out if what you are holding on to is nothing of value. When you figure out that much, then you know it's worth taking the risk.

Day 295

"I am neither especially clever, nor especially gifted, just very, very curious."

Albert Einstein

Interpretation: Question the norm and explore the alternative. That is when you have the best chance of stumbling upon the unexpected.

Day 296

"The difference between the impossible and the possible lies in a man's determination."

Tommy Lasorda

Interpretation: How determined you are, is the difference between possible and impossible. Those who are not determined at all obviously will not achieve the "impossible".

Day 297

"Again, you can't connect the dots looking forward you can only connect them looking backwards. So you have to trust that the dots will somehow connect in your future. You have to trust in something- your gut, destiny, life, karma, whatever. This approach has never let me down, and it has made all the difference in my life."

Steve Jobs

Interpretation: It might look like a mess right now, but each point in your life will lead you somewhere. Just trust in something that it will work out because when enough of the dots are laid, it will connect.

Day 298

"To achieve great things, you need a plan and not quite enough time."

Leonard Bernstein

Interpretation: Not having enough time creates a sense of urgency, which will make you take action. If we had all the time in the world, we would wait till tomorrow or the day after to start.

Day 299

"The thing with giving up is you never know. You never know whether you could have done the job. And I'm sick of not knowing about my life."

Sophie Kinsella

Interpretation: One of the worst things in life is not knowing what could've been especially if it's a decision whereby you are only held back by your wimpy fears.

Day 300

"You may have set-backs, and you may have failures, but you're not done - not by a longshot."

President Obama

Interpretation: Rarely does everything work out the way you plan and more times than not you will have set-backs. That's part of life, but all you have to do is keep on fighting.

Day 301

"Sometimes you just have to reach out and grab what you want, even when they tell you not to."

Rebecca Wells

Interpretation: I'm pretty sure she doesn't mean steal what you want even if it's illegal. But that there will be people who doubt you and tell you that you shouldn't go after what you want. Ignore them.

Day 302

"So I lost $25 billion. I started out with zero...no such thing as fear, not to an entrepreneur. Concern, yes. Fear, no"

Sheldon Adelson

Interpretation: We all started out with zero if you think about it. So, what if you quit your job and you lose all your money trying to start a business? Just go out there and find another job.

Day 303

"In order to succeed, your desire for success should be greater than your fear of failure."

Bill Cosby

Interpretation: Fear of failure holds you back like it shouldn't. But if you are able to overcome that fear, then you have a much better chance of succeeding.

Day 304

"Risks must be taken, because the greatest hazard in life is to risk nothing. The person who risks nothing, does nothing, has nothing, IS nothing. They may avoid suffering and sorrow, but they cannot learn, feel, change, grow, love and live."

Arnold Palmer

Interpretation: We can be safe and follow the norm. While this might have been great for survival centuries ago, it holds us back in today's society. You need to live life and that involves taking risks.

Day 305

"It isn't bad to want to get a degree, a good job, or a good reputation. But when wanting becomes craving, we are setting ourselves up for problems."

Roger Walsh

Interpretation: Everybody wants to be better, have a better job, be well-liked, and educated. That's a good thing, but when you push to extremes it will hurt your soul.

Day 306

"The only way to make real gains in your personal growth is to take action despite feeling timid, insecure, or fearful."

Brad Anastasia

Interpretation: Nearly everything I've done in life that was remotely worth it has been a result of facing a fear despite being scared out of my mind.

Day 307

"Our lives begin to end the day we become silent about things that matter."

Martin Luther King

Interpretation: Speak up if there is something that bothers you. Express yourself, especially if it is something you truly believe in.

Day 308

"It is easy in the world to live after the world's opinion it is easy in solitude to live after your own, but the great man is he who in the midst of the crowd keeps with perfect sweetness the independence of solitude."

Ralph Waldo Emerson

Interpretation: There will be naysayers and people who will tell you how to live your life. They will think they know what is best for you. It will be difficult, but try your best to do you.

Day 309

"It's not always easy to do what's not popular, but that's where you make your money."

John Neff

Interpretation: Follow the crowd and you are part of the crowd. Be the outlier and you will either be above the crowd or below it. But at least you give yourself a shot at the top.

Day 310

"If you don't fail you are not even trying."

Denzel Washington

Interpretation: This is a great pick me up when I see myself failing over and over again. But when that happens, it just means I haven't given up yet.

Day 311

"I want what all men want, I just want it more"

Achilles

Interpretation: How badly do you want something? If someone else wants it more than you, he or she might end up with it. Work hard.

Day 312

"The paradox of our time in history is that we have taller buildings but shorter tempers wider freeways but narrower viewpoints. We spend more but have less. We buy more but enjoy less. We have more degrees but less sense more knowledge but less judgment. We have multiplied our possessions but reduced our values. We talk too much, love too seldom, hate too often. We've learned how to make a living, but not a life."

George Carlin

Interpretation: We often get caught up with getting "more" and lose sight of what is important in life. Take a step back today and look through more open lens.

Day 313

"You're braver than you believe, and stronger than you seem, and smarter than you think."

A.A. Milne

Interpretation: Stay confident. When you think you can't, think you can. When you think you are weak, think you are strong. When you think you are ignorant, think you are smart.

Day 314

"I have been impressed with the urgency of doing. Knowing is not enough; we must apply. Being willing is not enough; we must do."

Leonardo da Vinci

Interpretation: Knowledge is just knowledge until it is applied. Potential is just potential until it is realized. Turn your knowledge and potential into action. That's where the value is.

Day 315

"Judge a man by his questions rather than by his answers."

Voltaire

Interpretation: Ask the right questions and you'll find the right answers. Intelligence is found when you analyze the questions versus the answers given.

Day 316

"That is the great American story: young people just like you, following their passions, determined to meet the times on their own terms...A willingness to follow your passions, regardless of whether they lead to fortune and fame."

President Obama

Interpretation: This is new American dream – following your passions and doing so on your own terms versus working in hopes of hitting it big or becoming famous.

Day 317

"You use all your vital energy on external things and wear out your spirit."

Chuang Tzu

Interpretation: Spend your energy trying to make money to buy more material possessions wears out your soul. Think more is less. Focus on that of which is important and cut out all other distractions.

Day 318

"If you want to improve be content to be thought foolish and stupid"

Epictetus

Interpretation: How you get better is by going through things you haven't experienced before. When you do that more likely than not you will be thought of as being foolish and sometimes even stupid.

Day 319

"It is not the man who has too little who is poor, but the one who hankers after more."

Seneca

Interpretation: The problem with wanting to be rich is that even after meeting your figure, you start to set another higher goal. This goes on and on and eventually you start feeling poor.

Day 320

"The best time to plant a tree was 20 years ago. The second best time is today."

an old proverb

Interpretation: Starting a business or a new career takes years and years of work to build into something valuable. Start now and 20 years from now, you'll have something amazing.

Day 321

"You just can't beat the person who never gives up."

Babe Ruth

Interpretation: Lesson from Babe Ruth is to never give up. Apparently you can't be beat if you never give up. I guess this means if you keep trying, you can't lose.

Day 322

"You have to look at what you have right in front of you, and what it could be, and stop measuring it against what you've lost."

Jonathan Tropper

Interpretation: This works in stock trading and it works in life. A loss is a loss and you can't get that back. What you can do is focus on what you have now and what that can become.

Day 323

"The simple compliments mean the most. Make someone's day."

Anonymous

Interpretation: That color looks good on you. I like your shoes. Those are only two of many compliments you can say to me if you bump into me today.

Day 324

"I think that everything is possible as long as you put your mind to it and you put the work and time into it. I think your mind really controls everything."

Michael Phelps

Interpretation: News flash? Most things are mental or fabricated in the mind. Overcome it in your mind and that will put you that much closer to coming out on top.

Day 325

"The more you can do to enjoy your life right now in the present, the less vulnerable you will be to disappointment from unmet expectations in the future."

Brad Anastasia

Interpretation: You know why you'll be less disappointed from unmet expectations in the future? Because you'll spend all your time thinking about the present; you won't have time to be disappointed.

Day 326

"I know it seems hard sometimes but remember one thing. Through every dark night there's a brighter day after that. So no matter how hard it get, stick your chest out, keep ya head up...and handle it."

Tupac

Interpretation: During Tupac's life, he battled with gangs, drugs, & violence. He came from nothing to become a great rap. If he says there's a brighter day after every dark night there is. Keep ya head up.

Day 327

"A man is a success if he gets up in the morning and goes to bed at night and in between does what he wants to do."

Bob Dylan

Interpretation: So does that mean if you have 9-5 job you would rather not go to you are not a success? Yes it does.

Day 328

"Years go by fast that it's hard not to think about the future. You live for the moment, of course, but you've also got to prepare for the future. That's life.

That's everybody. Being in the situation you're in now you definitely think about it, but you do live for the moment."

Lebron James

Interpretation: Personally, I' m not a Lebron James fan, but he pretty much hit this one on the spot. Live for the moment, plan for the future.

Day 329

"There are some defeats more triumphant than victories."

Michel de Montaigne

Interpretation: These defeats are the ones that make you stronger and even better prepared for the next battle. These defeats also humble you and allow you to respect your opponents or challenges.

Day 330

"The test of a first-rate intelligence is the ability to hold two opposed ideas in mind at the same time and still retain the ability to function. One should, for example, be able to see that things are hopeless and yet be determined to make them otherwise."

F. Scott Fitzgerald

Interpretation: If you are able to hold the two opposed ideas in your mind at the same time, you realize the difficulties the challenge presents but, are willing to give it a shot, or you just plain crazy.

Day 331

"Whatever I fear, I must face."

Steve Pavlina

Interpretation: Scared of getting rejected? Go for it anyways. Maybe you get rejected, or maybe you don't.

Day 332

"It is easy for the strong man to be strong as it is for the weak to be weak."

Ralph Waldo Emerson

Interpretation: Well of course it is easy for a strong man to be strong and a weak to be weak. That is what makes a strong man strong and a weak man weak. So which one are you – weak or strong?

Day 333

"You got a dream you gotta protect it. People can't do something themselves, they wanna tell you can't do it."

Gardner, to his son Christopher (Jaden Smith)

Interpretation: Of course if there is something someone else couldn't do, they would tell you that it can't be done. They don't want to be seen as failures or even worse, people who gave up too soon.

Day 334

"One half of knowing what you want is knowing what you must give up before you get it."

Sidney Howard

Interpretation: There's a common saying that you can't have it all. Remember if you want something there is always a trade-off. Is the risk worth the reward?

Day 335

"Believe you can and you're halfway there."

Theodore Roosevelt

Interpretation: Maybe this is too optimistic, but believing that you can is definitely the first step. Everything else follows that.

Day 336

"Courage is being scared to death, but saddling up anyway."

John Wayne

Interpretation: Be courageous today. Especially in front of your significant other. Trust me on this one. You won't regret it and you might even impress someone along the way.

Day 337

"Blessed are those who can give without remembering and take without forgetting"

Elizabeth Bibesco

Interpretation: Ideally, we want to give without expecting anything in return. Remember those who have given to you. Does this always happen? Of course not, but we can strive for this.

Day 338

"The world is like a pyramid of people struggling with one another. You don't have the choice of whether or not to join in the struggle, but you can choose where to fight"

Wealthy Man

Interpretation: Fight at the top where the competition isn't as rough and your odds of success are higher. Now you just need to figure out where the top of the pyramid is.

Day 339

"You never know how strong you are..until being strong is the ONLY choice you have."

Anonymous

Interpretation: You can wait until you are put in a situation where you have to be strong and that is the only choice, or you can create a situation that forces you to be strong.

Day 340

"Never try to be better than someone else. Always learn from others. Never cease in becoming the best you can be."

John Wooden

Interpretation: If you try to be better than someone else, you may cap yourself and sell yourself short. Basically the bar is that person. By being the best you can be, there is no limit to where you can go/be.

Day 341

"Take enough good swings at the ball and you'll get your hits."

Brett Steenbarger

Interpretation: The key here is good swings. Of course if you keep hitting poorly you may never hit the ball. Do enough right things and eventually some of those will start working out.

Day 342

"Good luck - you definitely made the right decision and you won't regret it, even if it doesn't work out the way you thought."

Seth Kugel on someone quitting his 9/5

Interpretation: A friend of mine quit his job without much of a net underneath him. Every once in a while I'll ask him if he regrets quitting his job. The answer is always the same, "I don't regret it".

Day 343

"Your training is my warm up."

Platz

Interpretation: This is what the Rock says to me when I'm working out. This is what I hope to say to those around me after I've worked on my fitness.

Day 344

"You will become clever through your mistakes."

German Proverb

Interpretation: Ever wonder how smart people get smart? They get smart by learning through their mistakes and also the mistakes of others.

Day 345

"When things get hard I think to myself easy day."

Jon Bones Jones

Interpretation: Quite frankly, it's all mental. Your hard day could be someone's easy day. As long as you keep telling yourself it's an easy day even if it is hard, you'll psyche yourself into thinking it's easy.

Day 346

"Don't measure yourself against other people, measure yourself against your own yardstick"

Royale Scuderi

Interpretation: Chances are your situation is different from someone else's, so measuring yourself against someone else is unfair and will likely result in inaccurate measurements. So why bother?

Day 347

"Eat a live frog first thing in the morning and nothing worse will happen to you the rest of the day."

Mark Twain

Interpretation: Well there aren't any frogs around me, but maybe I can count eating that plain tasteless oatmeal in the morning as the worst thing that will happen to me the rest of the day.

Day 348

"I've been absolutely terrified every moment of my life and I've never let it keep me from doing a single thing that I wanted to do."

Georgia O'Keeffe

Interpretation: Fear is a barrier. Overcome it and do things regardless of what you fear. Unless of course you know for a fact that it's not a good decision or could mean death.

Day 349

"I am an old man and have known a great many troubles, but most of them never happened."

Mark Twain

Interpretation: Most fears are fabricated in life, but there are also real fears like if you are at the zoo and a lion runs loose. I would be fearful for my life. Those are legitimate. But if you fear rejection...

Day 350

"When building your creation rituals, limit your bursts to no more than forty-five to ninety minutes, at least in the beginning."

Jonathan Fields

Interpretation: One thing I've learned with working on your own time is that you need to control your energy. It is hard to go hard for hours and hours on end. You need a break every once in a while.

Day 351

"We often use complexity for excusing ourselves from trying. Don't set out to build a castle; set out to lay a brick as perfectly as it can be placed. The castle will be built in the process."

Will Smith

Interpretation: Looking at the end result can be daunting. Break it into piece meal and take it one "brick" at a time. The end result will be the "castle".

Day 352

"Let us not pray to be sheltered from dangers but to be fearless when facing them."

Rabindranath Tagore

Interpretation: Danger will come sooner or later. Unless it is a tornado or hurricane, it's futile to be looking for shelter when danger comes. All else that is mental/psychological, you should face head on.

Day 353

"Predicting rain doesn't count, building arks does."

Warren Buffett

Interpretation: What good is a solution if you don't act on it? Anybody can suggest something or a route to take, but how many actually take action? Very few do so, therefore if you do, you'll stand out.

Day 354

"If there is any one secret of success, it lies in the ability to get the other person's point of view and see things from that person's point of view as well as from your own."

Henry Ford

Interpretation: In business and in life, you always want to put yourself in other's shoes. They might have a different view point than you, but it is worth seeing.

Day 355

"If you never take a risk you never get a reward"

Anonymous

Interpretation: No risk, no reward. If you want the prize, then go you'll have to be willing to take the risk. Sometimes if the reward is greater than the reward then it's a no brainer. Take the risk!

Day 356

"That's the most important thing. That's my message to the team is that you can't worry about the future, you can't worry about the past, you just have to focus on the present and we really have to maximize every single game."

Kobe Bryant

Interpretation: This is it and this is now. Work on the now and it will take care of the future. Focus on today when it's today and focus on tomorrow when its tomorrow.

Day 357

"The best way to predict the future is to create it."

Peter Drucker

Interpretation: Now if this only worked for a lottery ticket then I would be rich. But in all seriousness, your actions today will affect your future. Set yourself up for the future you are dreaming of.

Day 358

"The consistency you seek is in your mind, not in the markets. It is attitudes and beliefs about being wrong, losing money, and the tendency to become reckless, when you're feeling good, that cause most losses - not technique or market knowledge."

Mark Douglas

Interpretation: Stay disciplined in the decisions you make. In stock trading, wait for your trades to set up and then follow your trading plan to a T.

Day 359

"Manage your energy, not your time."

Tony Schwartz

Interpretation: We have 24 hours in a day, but we sleep for 8 hours of it. Make sure you have enough energy to get through the day and don't burn yourself out.

Day 360

"I am always doing that which I cannot do, in order that I may learn how to do it."

Pablo Picasso

Interpretation: Keep learning and doing things that you haven't done before. This will keep growing and expand your skill set.

Day 361

"If found nothing in life is worthwhile unless you take risks."

Denzel Washington

Interpretation: True statement. More often than not, if I don't take that risk presented to me, I regret it immediately.

Day 362

"The greater the obstacle, the more glory in achieving it."

Moliere

Interpretation: Do you remember how satisfying it was when you accomplished your last goal? Just remember the harder it is the more satisfying it is when you achieve it.

Day 363

"It's not just other people we need to forgive. We also need to forgive ourselves. For all the things we didn't do. All the things we should have done."

Mitch Albom

Interpretation: Forgive and forget. It might be hard to just let things go and for the perfectionist, it's almost impossible. But we need to forgive ourselves for our past mistakes. They only hold us back.

Day 364

"If your main goal in life is to escape worry, you are going to stay poor. You are also going to be bored silly. Life ought to be an adventure, not vegetation."

Max Gunther

Interpretation: The sooner you learn how to deal with worry and uncertainty, the better off you will be in life. That is unless of course you'd rather just vegetate until you die.

Day 365

"There is a voice inside of you that whispers all day long, I feel this is right for me, I know that this is wrong. No teacher, preacher, parent, friend or wise man can decide what's right for you - just listen to the voice that speaks inside."

Shel Silverstein

Interpretation: You can ask for all the advice in the world to make your "life-changing" decision. But, at the end of it all, you still need to make the decision on your own. Man up or woman up and decide.

About the Author

Kevin H graduated Cum Laude from University of California, Irvine with a Bachelors of Arts in Economics and Minor in Accounting. He is a Certified Public Accountant and has worked in a Big 4 public accounting firm (i.e. Ernst &Young, KPMG, Deloitte, or PwC) since 2009 primarily servicing clients in the credit services and life sciences/pharmaceuticals industries. However, he has experience in the automotive, electronics, and private equity industries as well. Prior to working in the Big 4, Kevin held a finance position at The Boeing Company.

Since 2005, he has been successfully trading stocks on the side - achieving high single digit to double digit returns each year. He combines fundamental analysis with technical analysis in determining which stocks to trade and when to trade them. His time frame ranges from days to three months.

This past year, he has written two other books Big 4 Accounting Audit - Interview Tricks & Tips and Essential Knowledge for a First Year Audit Staff/Intern at a Big 4 Accounting Firm, which you will be able to find on Amazon.com.

In addition, he also spent some time working at an investment banking firm, which focused on mergers and acquisitions. He is also the owner of www.StockKevin.com, a personal growth, stock trading, and financial savvy site. When he is not working, Kevin enjoys golfing, rock climbing, meditation, and yoga.